Inclusion in pre-school settings –
support for children with special needs and their families

Contents

Joseph concentrates on the dough, with active encouragement from Spider

All children have needs. They need a safe and secure environment in which to live and to play. They need interaction with known and trusted adults through which they can develop a framework for their own attitudes and behaviour.

Introduction

All children have needs. They need a safe and secure environment in which to live and to play. They need interaction with known and trusted adults through which they can develop a framework for their own attitudes and behaviour. They need the chance to explore their world, to learn about it and to discover their own place in it. They need opportunities to build up confidence and self-esteem by developing their full potential in all aspects of their life and learning. They need to be praised and encouraged for each step of their progress while being in no doubt that they are loved and valued for what they are now.

Early years settings must work towards meeting these needs for all the children in their care. For some children, adults may have to adjust the provision to a greater or lesser degree to ensure that the needs can be met, but the needs themselves remain the same.

The medical model

There have been various approaches to working with children with special needs. Until quite recently, children identified as having "special needs" were defined and categorised in terms of the disabilities/learning difficulties which made them different from other children and which were seen as needing to be "cured". This 'medical model', with its emphasis on difference, meant that their common childhood was sometimes in danger of being overlooked.

Inclusion

This book focuses instead on creating an "inclusive" approach in pre-schools. Inclusion works on the belief that all children have a right to be a part of their local community and to be welcomed and included on equal terms in their local pre-school. A pre-school aiming for an inclusive approach will be drawing on all available resources to create an environment within which each child can progress to her/his full potential in all areas of development.

An inclusive approach to education is just not a matter of making minor (or major) adjustments; inclusion is a process, which has to run through the whole curriculum if it is to be genuine. For example all the children, not merely those with identified special needs, need to see in the images presented to them in pre-school a world in which people with and without disabilities and learning difficulties have a contribution to make and things to offer one another. This has implications for the books in the book corner, the pictures on the wall and the range of adults who contribute as staff or visitors to the life of the group. All children – and all adults – should be able to find positive images of the group of people with whom they feel themselves to be identified. This includes issues of culture, ethnic group, age and gender, and also people's abilities/disabilities.

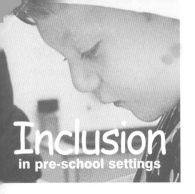

Inclusion
in pre-school settings

The Code of Practice

The Department for Education & Employment's Code of Practice on the Identification and Assessment of Special Educational Needs has been instrumental in supporting the move towards inclusiveness. Most pre-schools have long worked to the spirit of the Code and the Pre-school Learning Alliance actively supports its members in meeting the Code's more formal requirements. The charity's publication *Children with Special Needs in Pre-school – having regard to the Code of Practice*, published in 1997, looks at the Code's practical implications for pre-schools. This present book builds on that and replaces the earlier *Play and learning for ALL children*, showing ways in which pre-schools can support all of their children.

The organisation of the book

Although we are trying to move away from a medical model of disability, we have organised the book in terms of the areas of children's development and the ways in which their needs in these areas can be met in pre-school if their development is affected by illness or disability. This has been done to make it easier for people helping children with specific conditions to find what they want. However, all areas of development are interdependent, for children with and without special needs. Any attempt to arrange material in categories therefore soon encounters problems with overlap, as a condition with its roots in one area of development will very often have implications for others. We hope that the alphabetical presentation within each area of development will make the book and its contents more accessible, but we fully recognise that the classifications, like all attempts to classify people, are in some cases arbitrary. In order to avoid ambiguity, we have tried to use throughout the terminology adopted in the DfEE's Code of Practice.

No book on special educational needs could hope to be fully comprehensive. We have chosen to address in most detail the conditions which are most common among children in pre-schools, but have provided at the end an extensive resource list which will, we hope, be helpful to those needing more advice and information on specific conditions.

Working together

We very much hope that this book will be of help to people caring for children with special needs in a pre-school setting. However the first point of reference and advice will always be the child's parents. It cannot be said too often that although professionals in many fields have invaluable contributions to make to our understanding of conditions which affect children, the expert on the individual child is that child's parents. It is the parents who must mediate between professional services and the needs of the child. If they are to do this successfully, their expertise must be respected and their work supported within the group.

This can only happen if staff and parents work together in genuine partnership for the sake of the child, sharing each other's strengths and knowledge and supporting each other's weaknesses. This can mean a new approach on the part of the staff. They have to be willing to share knowledge and expertise, and also to learn new skills and fresh approaches. Changes in expectations and in working patterns can be a source of valuable stimulus and challenge to adults, but can also be stressful. On-going training, both within and outside the group, will give staff the confidence and satisfaction which come from extending skills and understanding, and will at the same time support them in making changes to their approach to both children and adults.

The value of pre-schools

The nature of pre-schools makes it easy for them to meet many of the aims of inclusion. The high adult:child ratios in pre-schools make possible an individual response to children; the ongoing training systems mean that adults' skills and knowledge are constantly updated; the active participation of parents sets a pattern for partnership; keyworker systems provide links with home and careful recording of the needs and progress of individual children. Above all, pre-schools are part of their local community, the focus very often of community involvement and support. . The pre-school model of society, in which all members have something to offer and in which all members can find the level of support they need, can provide an inclusive approach to the needs of all children.

Nico, who has a hearing impairment, makes excellent 'sausages' - and can count them too.

Children with sensory and neurological difficulties

Tracey has been blind from birth. She is a lively and intelligent little girl and her parents want to keep her in mainstream education. They have therefore been looking at their local pre-schools. They want one with an inclusive approach, but they also want one which uses a number of small rooms rather than one big one. Tracey will have to learn this new environment in order to move confidently in it, and her parents know from experience that she will orient herself more easily in smaller, more manageable spaces. Having found a group which can offer what they want, Tracey's parents then work with the staff and committee of the group to arrange that:

- *The room layout will be the same whenever Tracey attends*
- *Varied textures for items such as table covers provide information in a non-visual way*
- *Notices and labels, including name labels, are in Braille as well as using conventional writing/pictures*
- *Tracey's sessions in the group will begin with a guided 'feely' tour so that she can become familiar again with the resources on offer. Adults will then be alert to ensure that she is guided as appropriate to another activity/level of activity.*
- *At first, Tracey will be led by the hand from one room to another, counting the steps. Later, the accompanying adult will count without any physical contact. After a while, when Tracey feels confident enough, she will be able to go from room to room unaccompanied.*
- *The Early Years section of the local Partnership are approached for additional resource materials. Although the group already provides a rich environment, the pre-school staff and Tracy's parents feel that any additional materials which are available will enhance the provision, not only for Tracy herself but also for the other children.*

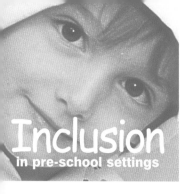

Children with cerebral palsy

Children with this condition have difficulty in controlling movement and/or balance, caused by the failure of one part of the brain to develop/work properly.

Children with this condition have difficulty in controlling movement and/or balance, caused by the failure of one part of the brain to develop/work properly. The failure can arise before birth, can sometimes be caused during birth and may also occur as a result of damage by meningitis or encephalitis. The effects range from mild weakness or lack of control in muscles to various levels of physical disablement, but the condition does not necessarily involve any loss of academic potential. One of the most frustrating aspects of cerebral palsy is that the physical symptoms can make it harder for other people to recognise and/or respond to indications of the child's intelligence. This in turn can sometimes impose an additional unnecessary disability. In an environment which works towards inclusion, the child must be supported - physically and in other ways - in doing everything that he or she can do or wants to attempt. Skill and sensitivity will be needed on the part of keyworkers and other staff to ensure that:

- a child who does not speak is nevertheless spoken to
- a child who is not able to approach activities is still actively encouraged and helped to join in them
- the physical aspects of pre-school activities are adapted as necessary to enable the child wherever possible to take part.

To help the child's physical safety and development, good posture is particularly important. All adults, including parents, need to model good practice for the child. This might include sitting up straight on a chair or standing straight with both feet on the floor. Adults might need practice themselves in doing this. Special furniture is available which helps children to align

themselves symmetrically to keep their balance correct and comfortable. If the child's condition has been diagnosed, appropriate equipment may be available via a therapist.

Some children with cerebral palsy will be on specific programmes such as conductive education. Groups will then need to work very closely with parents – and, where appropriate, with other professionals – to ensure that the child receives consistent messages.

Children with dyspraxia

This is not an easy condition to define or recognise, especially in the case of very young children, and it is possible that the pre-school will be the first place where the symptoms are recognised.

A combination of the following symptoms might suggest that the child may be suffering from dyspraxia:

- Lateness in reaching physical milestones of development
- The need to be taught 'simple' physical skills which other children seem to acquire spontaneously. These might include picking things up and putting them down in the right place, throwing things – from hand to hand or to another person, pedalling a tricycle
- Slowness and hesitancy in physical activity, including balancing
- The avoidance of mark-making or manipulative activities such as writing, drawing, painting, gluing, bead-threading, jigsaws.

If a child is showing a large number of these symptoms, the pre-school leader or keyworker will want to discuss with the child's parents whether the same problems are apparent at home. If this is the case, the pre-school may suggest to the parent that it would be worthwhile seeking medical advice, perhaps by a visit to the child development clinic or a discussion with the health visitor. Some parents may have been quite unaware that their child is struggling, but those with older children will probably have begun to suspect that there is something different about this child. They may be resistant to the idea or they may be grateful for the opportunity to discuss their anxieties.

If the condition is diagnosed, the group will need to maintain links with medical staff and/or an occupational therapist supporting the child.

Whether or not the condition has been diagnosed, the child must receive in an inclusive pre-school setting:

Experience of success

If an adult does the bulk of a difficult task, leaving the child to complete it, the child will gain some practice but also, more importantly, the confidence which comes from success. The child will then be motivated to try again, perhaps accomplishing a little more of the task next time.

Repetition

Children with dyspraxia need lots of practice in tackling activities and movements which may seem to come automatically to other children. If there is an obstacle course, for example, a child with dyspraxia will need to have lots of chances to go round it, especially if the challenges in the obstacle course include going through the tunnel, which some children with dyspraxia find very difficult.

Plenty of practice in co-ordination and balancing tasks

These might include threading, lacing and mark-making, dressing dolls, placing jigsaw pieces, screwing on and taking off lids and taking part in action rhymes and stacking games. These tasks will need to be made especially enjoyable in order to keep the child motivated.

Differentiation

It is especially important for these children that close and careful record-keeping ensures that the adults in the group, especially the keyworker, know exactly what the child has accomplished in order to provide the right support and encouragement in accomplishing the next small step.

Children with dyspraxia need lots of practice in tackling activities and movements which may seem to come automatically to other children.

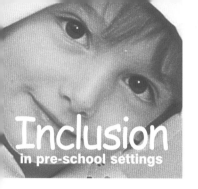

Children with hearing impairment

Despite the fact that screening is widely available for pre-school children, not all hearing loss will have been diagnosed before the child arrives in pre-school. This is particularly the case if the hearing loss is slight, recent or intermittent. These are some of the signs which might indicate imperfect hearing:

- Not responding to instructions, or not always responding to them, or responding to them partially or wrongly
- Communicating in a very noisy way, without apparently being aware of shouting or talking too loudly
- Not responding to or apparently enjoying stories unless they are supported by a lot of visual input
- Indistinct and/or delayed speech.

Any or all of these features, which may be more marked when the child has a cold, might make the adults in the group suspect some hearing loss. The parents should be approached and asked whether the child is experiencing similar difficulties at home. If the parents think there is any cause for anxiety they should approach their health visitor immediately and ask for a hearing test. They should not be deterred by the fact that the child may have had a test relatively recently. Some conditions can give rise to an intermittent hearing loss, so that whether or not the loss is picked up by the screening process depends upon whether or not the child happened to have good hearing on the day of the test.

In the pre-school, the activities offered to the child will aim to compensate for the loss of hearing and also to ensure that the hearing abilities the child does have are used, extended and supported in every possible way. It will be enormously helpful to all the adults and children in the group, but especially to those with hearing loss, if a listener-friendly environment can be created. This is an environment in which sounds can readily be heard and in which people find it easy to talk to one another. Features which can assist this are:

- As many soft surfaces as possible in order to absorb the noise which echoes off too many hard surfaces. Cushions, curtains, rugs and insulation materials are all helpful.
- An environment in which people do not raise their voices unnecessarily and in which people who speak are carefully listened to.
- Attention to unnecessary noise. Putting the nails for the woodwork bench in a non-metallic container can make a huge difference to overall noise levels. So can a few drops of oil on the axles of wheeled vehicles.

If the group is lucky enough to have a quiet room for books and stories, it may be possible to obtain grant aid to install an induction loop there.

Most of these environmental features will make the pre-school setting pleasanter and more conducive to concentration for all members of the group. As so often happens, good inclusive practice is also general good practice.

In music activities and when telling stories and singing songs, everybody needs to be especially careful to create links between sounds and visual images. This will help make things clearer for the child with hearing loss but it will also make songs and stories more vivid for many other children too. Stories can be accompanied by actions, story boards, puppets or other props. Songs also can be supported by pictures and actions.

Use the child's name, accompanied by a touch, to engage full visual attention before speaking to the group.

In the listening corner, there should be opportunities to respond to some loud sounds as well as quiet ones. A child with hearing loss may not be able to distinguish between the sounds made by a few grains of rice and a few lentils in a container, but might well be able to recognise the difference in sound and vibration between a handful of butter beans and a single conker. The child with a disability needs the same experiences as the other children, but a group aiming to create an inclusive environment will need to take more trouble to ensure that each child has opportunities to succeed.

Offering a combination of signing and speech can support the child in making connections between spoken words and meaning. If this is the approach which has been agreed, all adults in the group will need to learn the signing system, and to share it with the children:

- If the child has already been referred, a speech and language therapist may be able to advise.
- The health visitor may be able to recommend a local training source.
- The adult education college may run signing courses.
- The local branch of the Alliance may well have contacts.

The address of the Makaton Vocabulary Project is at the end of this book.

Some families very much want to concentrate on an approach based on spoken language. An organisation which can help with this is DELTA.

The address is at the end of the book.

The keyworker system, which benefits all children in the group, is of particular benefit to children with a special need. For a child with hearing loss, it is the keyworker very often who will be the first to know, for example, how the child's hearing aid works and how, if necessary, to adjust it. The keyworker will also be actively involved in observing and keeping records of the child's progress.

Moving to music can be deeply satisfying to children with hearing loss. The movement of the children who are moving in response to the music sends out vibrations which will allow the child who cannot hear the music, or can hear it only partially, nevertheless to enjoy joining in the response to it.

A child with a hearing loss can do almost everything that other children can do, and must be encouraged to do so. This includes not merely joining in the play activities but also taking an active and responsible part in the life of the pre-school. The child with a hearing loss has as much need and right as any other child to offer help to others, to make the playdough or mix the paint for the others, to help younger or smaller children and to be actively engaged in sharing and communicating.

Children affected by rubella

Children with visual impairment

Children damaged before birth by their mother's infection with the rubella virus may well be both blind and deaf. Children in this situation need a richly stimulating environment which enables them to take in as much information about the world as possible through their other senses. It is especially important to make use of the sense of touch. Children who cannot distinguish between objects or visual images by looking at their shape and colour need ample opportunities to distinguish between them on the basis of the way they feel. They need to encounter the same pictures, letters and numbers as other children, and the same opportunities to link them with other experiences and to distinguish between them, but for these children the distinctions will have to be made by touching. In an inclusive setting the environment will have to be adjusted to make this possible. For example, the group will need to provide resources which enable distinctions to be made, and shapes recognised, by tactile means. Organisations such as PLANET and SENSE may be able to provide opportunities and equipment and, since the child should be on the way to receiving a statement of special educational needs, the group will be maintaining close links with local authority support services.

Children with visual impairment are seldom without any vision at all, but may have very limited ability to see. Such children will be on the way to receiving, or may have received, a statement of special educational need and the group will work closely with the child's medical advisers and with local authority support services. They will need to work to provide the child with:

Confidence
Although for most children the group will aim for a flexible approach to the layout of equipment, responding to the need and opportunity of the moment, children with visual impairment need the confidence which comes from being able to know their way around the premises and the play equipment. It is helpful if, on the days when such a child attends, the layout can be almost always the same. If there have to be changes, the child should be guided through so that he or she knows what to expect.

Safety
It may be possible to protect children with visual impairment from unnecessary bumps and bruises by covering the corners of sharp-edged furniture with rubber strips or other padding. For children with some limited vision, reflective strips along the edges of furniture will help to guide them and protect them from bumps.

Sensory exploration
All children need this, and children with visual impairment need maximum opportunity to use the seeing ability they have as well as abundant stimulus for their other senses. There should be books with very bold, clear pictures for children who have any vision at all, together with plenty of light, both natural and artificial, but there should

also be opportunities to explore shapes, especially the shapes of letters and numbers, by means of textures or raised surfaces. Textured collage materials are a source of satisfaction to children with and without visual impairment.

Opportunities for physical play

Children with visual impairment have as much need to develop both large and small muscles as any other child, but the group may need to be more resourceful in ensuring that these children have as many opportunities to develop climbing and locomotion skills. A consistent layout, and care taken throughout the group not to leave dropped toys on the floor, will enable all children to use wheeled vehicles safely. Sturdy cubes will provide opportunities for climbing and scrambling and also for experiencing sensations of enclosure and the co-ordination needed to ascend and descend steps. The child's keyworker will need to keep a very careful balance between putting the child at risk of bumps and bruises and limiting the child's physical development by being unduly cautious or helpful.

Opportunities to read and write

A child with very limited vision will need to learn Braille and dual-language books are now available in Braille/non-Braille text. These can be loaned from a project called Clear Vision and since the child may have a statement it is a good idea to ask the local authority library to join. The address is at the end of the book.

Self-esteem

One of the things which supports children's self-esteem in pre-school is the evidence that they are part of a group: their name on a peg, their named work displayed on the wall, pictures of them drawn by other children, their own familiar name and symbol around the neck of a milk bottle at the snack table. These opportunities for developing self-esteem and self-confidence are not so readily available to the child with a visual impairment and an inclusive environment must aim to "bridge the gap". The same practical ends can be achieved, and the child's self-esteem boosted, by ensuring that the name and/or picture are created in relief, or by means of textured materials, and that textured displays of this kind are within the child's reach, not just at adult eye-level. When the children in the group are creating books or pictures about things they like, the child with limited vision may need opportunities to cut shapes, or have them cut, out of felt or velvet to make a similar book.

The other resources in the pre-school should acknowledge the child's disability if possible, making it clear to all the members of the group that people with disabilities are an ordinary part of the world: provide glasses (without lenses) for the dolls; ensure that stories are sometimes about children with a disability; consider buying one or more of the dolls specially made to represent people with specific disabilities. (It is possible for example to buy dolls with white sticks.)

In an inclusive environment, children with physical and sensory disabilities need to be given responsibility, both for themselves and where appropriate for other people. They can meet the same standards of behaviour as other children, can be helpful and supportive to their friends and can make practical contributions to the life of the group, and they must be encouraged and supported in order to ensure that they do so.

"An environment which is attractive to children" - Grace enjoys the ball pool.

Children with emotional and behavioural difficulties

The pre-school leader tries to persuade Lucy to join her at the dough table, but Lucy spits at her and heads rapidly across the room to the construction area, where Carlos is building with the wooden blocks. Lucy demolishes the construction with one swipe of her hand and, as Carlos moves to protest, hits him with one of the blocks.

Leon has not managed to make the pieces of card he was sticking hold together in the way he had intended. He has put down the spatula and is standing rigid and trembling with anger. Adults see his distress and attempt to comfort him but he will not allow anyone to come near him. He withdraws from the activity, standing with his back to the wall looking on. He makes no response to approaches by other children and physically withdraws whenever an adult attempts to touch or speak to him. He has no friends in the group.

These two situations illustrate two aspects of behavioural difficulty, one "acting out" through aggressive and disruptive behaviour and one "acting in", being isolated, anxious and withdrawn.

It is tempting to label as "behavioural difficulty" any behaviour which appears inappropriate – or even inconvenient – to adults. However, behavioural and/or emotional difficulty can better be defined as a pattern of behaviour, or even a single action, which interferes with the learning, development or happiness of a child or of the group of which the child is a part, or with adult attempts to promote learning and friendship. The continuum of emotional and behavioural difficulty ranges from behaviour which may challenge adults but remains within the normal range to behaviour which may be associated with some form of disturbance.

Work with children who have a behavioural/learning difficulty will rest on careful observation of the child in question, and the keeping of accurate, objective records of what has been observed. If Leon's keyworker notices, for example, that he sometimes hums to himself when he needs comfort, s/he might attempt the strategy of approaching him by means of a favourite song.

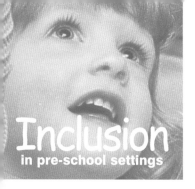
Symptoms which might alert adults to the existence of an emotional or behavioural difficulty include:

- Not concentrating
- A destructive approach to other children's activities
- Physical and/or verbal aggression towards other children and/or adults
- Unwillingness or inability to accept the discipline of adults
- Inability to make or receive emotional attachments
- Over-dependence on adults
- Excessive shyness
- Tantrums
- Hyperactivity.

Many of these symptoms can be caused by short-term problems such as family disruption, bereavement, moving house or separation. However, some combinations of symptoms can also have other more fundamental causes, such as abuse, neglect, communication difficulty, sensory impairment or physical or mental illness. Similar symptoms might also appear in a child who is not used to consistent handling and boundaries, or who has not yet learned to play socially with other children.

The child in the family
Symptoms of emotional and behavioural disorder will very often be picked up at home by the child's parents and other carers. If record-keeping is shared with parents, or if keyworkers are careful to give parents regular opportunities to share their knowledge, parents might report that:

- The child is "destructive"
- They cannot safely trust the child with other children or the new baby
- The child will not sleep
- The child has feeding difficulties
- The child is or seems to be very different in his or her behaviour and emotional attitudes from the other children in the family.

Support through the pre-school
Pre-schools need to agree a three-stage strategy with regard to the challenging behaviour which can arise from emotional and behavioural difficulty:

Prevention
An environment which is attractive to children, and organised so as to offer interesting and differentiated resources and activities, can help children to find acceptable ways to behave and to express their feelings.

General strategies for dealing with unacceptable behaviour
Tactics will range from strategically ignoring some behaviour to offering simple choices and making very clear the consequences of unacceptable behaviour. (Any person who throws sand, for example, is automatically taken away from the sand table.) The group will aim to become sensitive to events which can "trigger" unacceptable behaviour and to ensure that the behaviours they want to encourage are amply rewarded.

Handling individual examples of unacceptable behaviour
This will arise from knowledge of the individual child, but will usually include establishing eye contact, using very positive language – and very simple language if the child has a limited

vocabulary – and finding also something to praise if possible. It is very important to ensure that the behaviour is handled consistently, so that the child will learn where the boundaries are.

The pre-school staff will work together as they would for any child to develop an individual education plan based on close observation of the child. Whether or not children are in process of being assessed under the Code of Practice, they need to be given specific targets, together with appropriate support in meeting them.

The difficulties presented by any individual child at any one time will be peculiar to that child and that situation, and must be approached on an individual basis. However, in general terms, the following methods can be used to offer maximum support to children with specific emotional and behavioural difficulties:

A child who cannot concentrate
Identify by observation the child's own interests and strengths. Build on these, offering praise, additional resources and individual adult support gradually to extend the child's ability to concentrate on a specific activity. Reward success in concentrating for longer periods, involving the child in setting targets.

A child whose approach to other children's activities is destructive
It needs to be clear that, while the child is welcome and wanted, the behaviour is unacceptable. The child should have close and constant adult supervision. The adult supervising will also ensure that the child has plenty of things to do – things which are meaningful to the child – and adult support if necessary in pursuing them. If one child destroys or damages another child's work, an adult will talk to the child causing the damage in order to try to explain what is wrong with what s/he has done. Some children with emotional and behavioural difficulties have limited language skills. For them, explanations and prohibitions must be simple, clear, repeated as necessary and supplemented by signing as necessary.

It is important to use positive rather than negative language when talking to the child about what has been happening. Encouragement, for example, to build a tower alongside Jonathan's is better than an instruction not to knock down Jonathan's tower.

For some children it can be helpful to provide for legitimate destruction: large cardboard boxes to break up, large lumps of clay to pound, big sheets of paper to colour in strong colours, buildings constructed by the child – with adult help if necessary – which can then be destroyed if the child wishes. Physical challenges, such as pushing barrow loads of clay or sand, can also help to defuse the build-up of emotional energy which can result in destructive behaviour.

Physical and verbal aggression
Once again it needs to be made clear that such behaviour is never acceptable, but that the child herself or himself is still welcomed and a valued part of the group and that adults will work with her or him to make the necessary changes in behaviour. This will involve close and constant supervision, partly to protect the child from making mistakes and partly to ensure that all instances of positive behaviour are promptly and warmly praised and rewarded. It may be necessary for the group to structure situations which enable the child to play with other children. Equipment which requires two people to use it satisfactorily – such as some of the very large

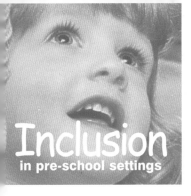

wheeled vehicles made by Community Playthings – can be helpful. The adult will need to work with both children to ensure that the sharing and co-operation work successfully, otherwise the result could be one more negative message for the child.

Many groups have policies on equal opportunities which require that any verbal aggression which takes the form of sexist or racist abuse must be tackled promptly, the victim comforted and the aggressor helped to understand what was wrong. Implementation of these policies can be accomplished while working to support a child with emotional and behavioural difficulties. Temporary withdrawal in company with an adult will provide an opportunity to talk through what has gone wrong while making it clear to all others in the group that behaviour of this kind is never acceptable.

A child who will not accept adult authority

The first requirement here is to ensure that the rules in the pre-school are as few as possible, clearly understood by all children and consistently enforced by all adults. The adults in the staff team and the management committee need to be clear about what is most important and to limit the rules to essentials. If many of the rules seem to be designed simply to keep children safe, it may be that the group needs to look afresh at its equipment and layout in order to create a safe environment that does not rest upon too many regulations.

It is very difficult for children to keep the rules if they do not understand them or the thinking behind them. Some groups ensure that the rules are written as part of the introductory leaflet prepared for newcomers and discussed between parents and keyworker before the child joins the group. It is then possible for the child's parents to talk through with the child before attending the group the kinds of behaviour which will be required there. This also gives an opportunity for discussion in advance if there appears to be any conflict between the rules of the group and the behaviour which is expected or encouraged at home.

A child who does not obey

If a child appears to ignore instructions, it is wise to check first that these have been heard and fully understood. Some children have mild hearing loss on some frequencies, and some children have an intermittent hearing loss associated perhaps with catarrhal infections. Others have genuine difficulty in attending to more than one thing at once. It is confusing and unjust for a child to be accused of disobedience when he or she has not been able to "take on board" any instruction given. It is important also for adults to be sure that the instructions they give are absolutely clear to all children. The vocabulary and intonation used by adults in pre-school may be very different from that which is familiar to them at home. This can make it hard initially for children to know what is expected of them. Some children will need a name and a touch before an instruction is given to ensure that they are attending to it.

Sometimes disobedience is an expression of a child's developing – and legitimate – need for autonomy. It is helpful to ensure that the pre-school activities and equipment are presented in such a way that children have opportunities to select and to follow through their choice in the knowledge that their decisions will be respected and supported by the adults. Even in a situation in which there is very limited choice for a child, an instruction can be phrased in such a way that the child is required to endorse a desirable course of action. If a child is simply told to sit down, for example, he or she may refuse. If the instruction is re-worded as a choice: "Do you want to sit down on the chair or on the mat?" the response is more likely to be a positive one. Instructions phrased in a way which involves several people, as an invitation rather than a command – "Let's all sit down" – are less likely to trigger an unacceptable response. Another non-threatening way to phrase an instruction is to make a song of it: "This is the way we sit on the chairs" fits to the tune of *"Here we go round the Mulberry Bush"* and "Sit down, Janine" can be sung to *"Frère Jacques"*.

Some children benefit from close adult company, not merely to provide supervision but to support the child in attempts to change behaviour and to protect her or him from slipping back into behaviour which will cause trouble.

A child who makes no attachments
A child who is withdrawn from adults and other children often needs initially a lot of reassurance, which can be provided by a familiar structure and routine in the group as well as by plenty of smiles, eye contact, friendly gestures and the giving of objects and sometimes food. It is important to praise what the child can do rather than criticise her or him for failure to do other things. Consistent handling of behaviour is especially important for these children, combined with positive language and generous praise for success. Adults can structure the beginning of an approach to other children by setting up paired interactions, preferably based upon a fairly emotionally neutral activity such as a board

game. Very withdrawn children will find it too hard, at least initially, to take part in group co-operative play and will need one keyworker or "attachment figure" to relate to at first.

A child who is too dependent
These children, like many others, will be helped by a very gradual settling-in procedure at the pre-school, at a pace that both child and parent can comfortably handle. A previous visit to the child's home can be helpful, to enable the child to see the new adults in a familiar setting and to feel that they are endorsed by the child's home and parents.

Many children find it helpful to build up a relationship with a "transitional" adult, whose friendship can act as a bridge between parents and the unfamiliar pre-school setting. This will usually be the child's keyworker. Whoever this person is, it is particularly important that she/he be available to the child at moments of stress. For most young children these include the beginning and end of the day/session and also any large group activities such as circle-time, snack-time or large group singing sessions.

One way to ease the separation from parents or familiar carers is to provide immediate distraction. To have a favourite and undemanding activity within easy reach of the door can make it possible for a very dependent child to take the first step into the room and to become absorbed in an activity.

It will help to set up situations in which paired interaction, preferably with an older or more mature child, is possible. At first it is likely that the dependent child will simply play alongside the other child in the company of a familiar adult.

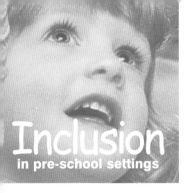
Once this situation is accepted, the adults can initiate more active sharing. It may be suggested for example that one child holds up the piece of tubing so that the other can pour coloured water into one end. Stories and rhymes in very small groups can also be helpful, as they enable the child to share a response with other children without being in a group whose size makes demands which the child cannot yet meet.

A familiar structure to the pre-school session will help a child who finds it hard to be away from parents/carers to cope with the situation by recognising the progress of time and being able to anticipate when parents can be expected to reappear. Many children can cope with a diagram or pictures showing in sequence the order of events in the pre-school session, and there is no reason why this should not be shared with them as well as with staff, parents and helpers.

Some children are greatly helped by having with them concrete links with home. For some children this involves refusing to take off the coat which they have put on at home. This should be accepted for as long as necessary. Some children find the same comfort in familiar toys or other objects brought from home. More dynamic links with home can be created by the active involvement of parents and family in the pre-school's themes and activities. Sharing with parents a search at home for items to contribute, for example, to an interest table or themed display can help the child build a bridge between home and pre-school and make separation easier to bear.

It should go without saying that the key to helping the child to settle is the child's parent.

Parents must be fully involved with the process of settling and separation, their advice sought and valued, and it must be clear to them that they are absolutely welcome and indeed necessary in the group for as long as the child needs them there.

Parents, like children, bring to the group their own particular needs, problems and attitudes. Some, desperate for a break from a demanding child, or needing time to earn money, may see the group as a childcare facility rather than as a shared commitment to the child's progress. Others may be reluctant to part from a child they see as needing their constant protection, or afraid at their own loss of function as the child grows up. Meetings and information before the child begins to attend the group can clear up any misunderstandings and can also offer parents a range of ways of being involved – in the group itself and in their individual child's progress.

An excessively shy child

For these children also a transitional adult, one who can create a bridge between home and pre-school, can be a means of helping the child to begin to make social contacts. From all adults in the group the child will need quiet, on-going friendliness and reassurance.

Adults will need to take responsibility for ensuring that the child is gradually exposed to opportunities to make relationships with less familiar adults and with other children and also to tackle a widening range of activities. Adults have to be lavish with praise and encouragement, recording and celebrating the steps the child makes, however small they are.

Tantrums

This total loss of control is not uncommon among toddlers. It is triggered often by the child's frustration at being unable to make people – or things – accord with her/his wishes, combined with a lack of vocabulary for expressing the powerful emotions aroused. As with many aspects of emotional and behavioural difficulty, behaviour which is acceptable in a baby or very young child gives rise to concern if it occurs later on. The techniques for handling the situation, however, remain the same:

- Provide the child with the security of an adult who will not himself/herself lose control.
- Prevent actual damage, to the child, other children or property, using a hug if necessary as a form of restraint, so long as other adults are present to witness it.*
- Do not reproach the child; a genuine tantrum is not within the child's control.
- Once the tantrum is subsiding, provide distraction. A quiet activity shared with an adult can help.
- Observe the child closely. It may be possible to protect the child from a tantrum by spotting "trigger" situations and defusing them in advance.
- Take active steps to build up the child's vocabulary, and other media of expression, so that s/he can begin to take charge of emotion and express it in other ways.

A child who is hyperactive - and who may have been diagnosed as having attention deficit disorder (ADD) or attention deficit hyperactive disorder (ADHD)

A child who cannot settle to any activity needs close and constant supervision, partly to keep her or him from disrupting the rest of the group but partly also to protect the child from getting into trouble and to help the child work towards agreed targets in terms of concentration, social behaviour and remaining "on task" for increasing periods.

It is important for adults working with these children to remember to use positive language and to encourage them to do things rather than not to do things. Close observation and record-keeping will enable adults in the group to be aware of the child's interests and skills and these should be built upon, both to promote the child's own self-esteem and self-confidence and to provide a distraction when necessary from less desirable activities. The child himself/herself should be involved in the setting of targets and rewarded for progress towards them. Children who show very high levels of activity can make considerable progress if the activities which are presented to them are sufficiently differentiated, so that the child can encounter an activity at a level he or she can cope with and can then be helped to go on to approach it in an increasingly demanding way. At the simplest level, a child who usually makes one mark on the paper before abandoning the painting area can be encouraged to make two marks in the same colour, then two marks in different colours, which involves putting down one brush and picking up another one. Each of these small steps can be praised and shared with parents before another "target" is set.

Some children who are very active need to avoid certain foods or additives. Staff should ensure that they have up-to-date information on this from the child's parents and/or health visitor.

---

* The DfEE have issued guidelines on the use of restraint.

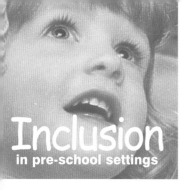

Inclusion
in pre-school settings

Strategies for adults to use

In a situation where strong feelings are involved, any adult intervention strategy must be adopted and used with great caution, especially any strategies which involve physical contact with the child:

- Physical restraint, in the form of a controlling hug, can be helpful, but must always be witnessed by another adult.*
- Many groups have a rule that a child who cannot play appropriately with the activities provided must withdraw from them for a while. This withdrawal should always be in the company of an adult and should be regarded not as a penalty but as an opportunity for adult and child together to consider what went wrong and how things should be handled next time. This joint withdrawal should always be arranged in such a way that another adult can witness it.

Strategies such as these will be used with care, agreed in advance by all staff and known to the parents through the group's policies and procedures on behaviour.

All the adults involved in the group in any way – including those who come in on a short term basis – need to know what the rules are and what their part must be in enforcing them. This makes meetings amongst the adults, especially the staff team, very important. All the adults involved must be confident about the rules and the thinking behind them, and should express them in an agreed way.

It takes self-discipline on the part of the staff and helpers to create a firm, fair and consistent pattern within which all children know what to expect and all children clearly understand that some kinds of behaviour will be automatically followed by, for example, removal from that activity. Without this, children will find it very hard to believe in the rules and may well experiment in order to establish where the limits of acceptable behaviour really are.

The adults must take great care to give clear messages to the children. If a particular kind of behaviour is unacceptable, for example, the adults need to show it – not just in words, but in body language and tone of voice. Mixed messages will confuse the children and may prolong the unwanted behaviour. For young children with reduced language ability, the signals need to be few and very clear.

We often underestimate young children's capacity to understand and think about rules and the need for them. Rules which the children have discussed together, whose purpose they understand and endorse, are more likely to be followed, and pressure from peers as well as from staff will help children who have difficulty in conforming.

Contacts

In addition to routine contacts with health visitors, social services and the LEA educational psychology service, it would be useful to make links with national voluntary organisations offering support for specific conditions, such as the National Autistic Society and the National ADD/ADHD (Attention deficit disorder, with or without hyperactivity) organisation, which now has its own website.

* The DfEE have issued guidelines on the use of restraint.

The needs of the group

Children with emotional and behavioural difficulties can impose great stress on the other members of the group, both children and adults.

For children, concentration, learning and pleasure may be disrupted by noise, inappropriate behaviour or even physical attacks.

For adults, there is the strain of having to be constantly on the alert to handle a situation which they know may be contained or improved by their actions but probably not ever "solved". There are also the conflicts of interest and commitment which arise when their concern for the child with behavioural difficulties is complicated by their equal concern for the other children in the group. Some of these may become distressed and fearful and there is always the danger that their parents may then remove them, threatening the continued success and sometimes the very existence of the group.

The group must set up systems which allow the adults to provide maximum support for one another. They may need:

- Time to share problems, agree approaches and review progress
- Sufficient numbers of staff to allow them to take turns, each having an occasional break from the most stressful situations
- To establish priorities. A child presenting several forms of unacceptable behaviour cannot be expected to tackle them all at once, and to try to do so creates feelings of failure. If the whole group decides to concentrate on just one aspect of a child's behaviour, putting the rest "on hold" as far as possible, both child and staff are more likely to be rewarded by some small success, which then provides the motivation and confidence to move on to the next thing.

Sometimes, deep breathing can help – for the adult and also for the child presenting difficulties.

Children – and adults – with emotional and behavioural difficulties need an approach which is both tolerant and respectful. They must be sure at all times that they themselves are valued and welcome even though their behaviour may need to change. For all children whose behaviour needs to change, there should be a series of small, attainable targets, shared with the parents and the child as well as with all adults in the group. Successes likewise should be shared with all concerned, and celebrated with the child.

Signing provides an additional language resource.

Children with speech and language difficulties

Darren listens eagerly to the story in pre-school. Other children at the end contribute their own comments and experiences. Darren, however, although clearly wanting to join in, cannot make any contribution until the pre-school leader encourages him to hold one of the puppets from the story bag she is using. This enables him to relax and join in the discussion despite his stammer.

"It is time to come and sit on the mat now," says the pre-school leader. Michelle smiles at her obligingly, then goes back to the blocks and continues to arrange them.

Speech and language delay or difficulties can take many forms. Children who are encountering difficulties may demonstrate:

- An inability or unwillingness to express ideas in speech
- Lack of vocabulary or lack of understanding of the words used
- The inability to speak coherently
- The inability to regulate voice tone or voice level, or to pronounce specific sounds
- Failure to listen to or respond to other people's speech
- General difficulty in communicating with adults and other children by means of ordinary conversation
- Progress through the ordinary stages of language acquisition but at a much slower rate than other children.

Many factors can affect children's speech and language development. Problems may be caused by:

- Developmental delay
- One or more medical/physiological conditions
- Emotional or social issues
- Autistic spectrum disorders (See page 42)

Support through pre-school

The supportive environment of a pre-school, with a high adult:child ratio and a keyworker system ensuring individual attention to the development and needs of each child, can often be a means of providing the support which children and families need.

These are some of the areas in which children can encounter difficulties:

Communicating

It is easy to forget that communicating with one another is a very complicated and sophisticated skill. It involves:

- Following what another person is saying
- Recognising that people have to take turns to speak
- Understanding that the second person to speak needs to respond to what the first speaker has said, rather than introducing something completely different
- Waiting until other people have finished speaking.

Many children who start pre-school have already learned to do these things, but some have not had opportunities to learn about conversation at home. Others may have been exposed to lots of talk at home but may not yet have learnt to join in. In pre-school, adults will offer a model of conversational techniques:

- Using language not just to offer commands but to share experiences and ideas
- Maintaining eye contact while speaking to people
- Modelling courtesies such as turn-taking
- Providing silences in which children are free to add their own comments and responses.

It can be hard for many children to understand when responses and comments are appropriate and when they are not. Children who break into the middle of conversation or interrupt in the middle of a story have to be helped to behave differently without discouraging their own attempts at speech, but also without spoiling the shared experience for other children. Use of the child's own name can be a useful way of acknowledging the child's input and steering the situation: "Yes, that's exactly right, John. Sit down and I'll tell you all what happened next."

It is not possible to conduct conversations if there is nothing to talk about. Some children arrive in pre-school eager to tell the staff about what has been happening at home. Other children can find no bridge between their home experiences and the situations and vocabulary available to them in the pre-school. For these children it is particularly important to provide in pre-school shared experiences, especially small outings, themes, projects or visitors, about which staff and children can talk to one another. Photographs of such events can be a useful tool in helping children to recollect and talk about what happened and what they did.

Expressive language

All children need to be able to learn to use language to express their feelings. In order to do this, they have to understand:

- That the feelings they experience are experienced also by other people; that there is a name for them and that if they use that name other people will understand what they mean
- That there is nothing wrong with their feelings in themselves, and that expressing them in language is often the most appropriate and acceptable way to express them.

To accomplish this, the books and stories provided for children need to include some which support children in recognising and naming feelings, ideas and emotions. Libraries and publishers committed to challenging stereotypes with regard to culture, gender and ethnic group are often also a useful source of books about feelings. Try Letterbox Library (address at end). Observant adults must also be able to recognise from the children's behaviour how they are feeling and be able to feed back to them the vocabulary they need: "I know you're feeling angry because Susan knocked your bricks over"; "I know you all feel disappointed because the rain has stopped us going to the park"; "I know you're excited because your birthday party is this afternoon." This provides children with the vocabulary they need and an acknowledgement that the way they feel is valid and accepted.

Some children do not speak. It may not be clear at first whether this is because they cannot speak or because they are refusing to do so. In either case, gestures and signing, both accompanied by speech, can provide necessary help:

- For a child who cannot speak, signing provides a necessary means of communication.
- For other children, linking signing to speech

provides a bridge to communication. Such children may begin by signing and then, if the signs of the adults are constantly accompanied by speech, start to speak themselves.

- Introduce just a few key signs at first
- For children who talk at home but elect to be silent in the group, a home visit by the keyworker can help "break the ice" by creating a link between the two settings.

Receiving language

Some children cannot hear, or cannot hear clearly, or cannot hear some sounds, or cannot hear all the time. This may become apparent when children:

- Appear to disregard adults' instructions
- Do not respond to sounds or activities to the side or behind them
- Show loss of attention when required to respond to storytelling or other spoken stimulus
- Respond or obey on some occasions and not others.

Adults can help such children to make connections between speech and meaning by accompanying speech by signing and by ensuring that when they talk to the child they are always fully facing the child so that they gradually build up connections between sounds and facial gestures.

Children who are not receiving enough sound stimulus need a very strong visual environment. Activities need to be supported as much as possible by visual cues. Story time, for example, can be supported by the use of story sacks, story boards, puppets and pictures. Singing time can have large clear pictures illustrating songs or rhymes. All visual cues need to be displayed very clearly and at the child's own eye level.

Music and movement can be a liberating experience for children whose hearing is limited. The vibrations set up by the other children's clapping and stamping can provide necessary links between sound, movement and gesture so that children whose hearing is very limited can still join in and gain pleasure from a physical response to rhythm.

Stammering

This can be made worse by tension or anxiety in the child. Adults need to create a calm and relaxing environment within which the child can speak at his or her own pace without stress:

- Speak slowly and calmly in order to keep the atmosphere relaxed.
- Wait, without showing signs of anxiety, irritation or impatience.
- Do not correct the child's speech or finish the sentence, however long it takes.
- Smile. Make it clear that this is a conversation you are enjoying and want to take part in.
- Give the child physical comfort and reassurance, such as by taking the child's hand, if this is appropriate and helpful for that particular child.

Speech quality

Some children find it very difficult to control what kind of noise they make when they are speaking. Their voices may be much too noisy, inappropriately articulated, or almost inaudible.

The problem may be a medical one, and medical advice should be sought. In addition, there are practical things the adults can do in pre-school:

- For children who find difficulty in making sufficient noise, keep the noise down in the group by providing carpets, cushions, beanbags and any other kinds of soft substances to absorb sound.

- Accompany speech by signing so that children who find communicating by speech very difficult and burdensome can learn another mode of communication.

- Be aware that for children who use signing, the gestures which accompany traditional finger-rhymes can sometimes be a source of confusion because the children are then, in effect, using two different "signing" systems at once.

- Introduce a range of songs in which the child can take part on an equal basis: songs in which some words or verses are to be whispered; others shouted.

- Provide some games and activities in which speech is simply irrelevant, so that the child can take part and take pleasure in the play and learning without being exposed to the stress of constantly attempting a very difficult or impossible task. Playing with construction equipment, paint or malleable materials such as dough or clay can be done and enjoyed without speech, and children who find speech difficult should have a chance to be praised for their accomplishments in other areas.

Articulation disorder
Some children find it difficult to make one or more specific sounds. The problem may be physiological; it can also be an emotional problem and may occasionally be cultural. All human languages draw upon a slightly different range of sounds and a child brought up in a culture which does not use a particular sound may have difficulty in using it later on. A common example of this is the traditional problem experienced by English people trying to roll their Rs in French.

Advice from the doctor or speech and language therapist may include recommendations for particular games to play with the child. Some activities, however, will be helpful for all children who have difficulty in articulating:

- In conversation with the child, feed back the correct version of what he or she has been saying without overtly correcting or contradicting the child. "I like 'au'age." – "Yes, I know you do. You ate a lot of sausage at lunchtime."

- Provide games which involve using the muscles of the mouth, tongue and throat: blowing bubbles; playing "football" with table tennis balls on a table; pretending to lick jam from around their mouths (this can be done as part of songs such as *Here we go round the Mulberry Bush*"; encouraging parents to let the child play a blown instrument at home such as a recorder, penny whistle or ocarina.

Speech problems arising from learning difficulties
Some children either do not understand the speech they hear or, understanding it, cannot make themselves understood. When looking after babies, adults expect that there will be problems with both speech and understanding and automatically use techniques which will assist the baby to develop the necessary skills for communicating by language:

- Speaking always very slowly and clearly, facing the child from a close range
- Making very clear the links between words and meaning, for example by naming objects while pointing to them or by introducing the words for concepts such as *big/small* or *full/empty* as relevant during the child's play
- Listening very carefully so as to give meaning to the sounds the child is making
- Using very simple language.

All of these techniques will work with, or help, older children who are going through the same developmental stages as a much younger child.

Children need to be helped to be aware of what their own facial muscles can do. Games with facial expressions, which can be included in "Simon says" activities, will help children to be conscious of what they can do with facial muscles as well as introducing them to the social implications of facial expression.

Children who are having difficulty in expressing themselves by means of language need other modes of expression. For these children, activities such as dancing, painting and modelling with clay or recycled "junk" materials become doubly important.

Words become particularly vivid when they are attached to experiences which have meaning for the child. Vocabulary can be extended most readily by giving names to objects which are important to the child and by labelling experiences which have become vivid for the child by means of individual activities. Prepositions such as "in", "through" and "under", for example, can be most readily introduced in connection with children's play as they post themselves through holes, enclose themselves in boxes and wriggle under mats.

Outside contacts

Speech is a key part of all human life, and the work of the pre-school in helping children to express themselves in language must be co-ordinated with the families' efforts in the same direction.

Speech therapists are very hard to come by in many parts of the country, but the Royal College of Speech and Language Therapists provides notes for parents of children experiencing speech and language difficulties and these make a good basis for providing a joint plan of action between parents and pre-school.

The Makaton Vocabulary Development Project is an essential resource for groups and individuals wishing to use signing. Other useful voluntary agencies dealing with aspects of children's speech and language development include Afasic (Unlocking speech and language), I CAN (schools and nurseries for children encountering major difficulties in speech and language) and the British Stammerers' Association. Addresses are at the end of the book.

Reluctance or refusal to speak can sometimes be a symptom of general withdrawal on the part of the child. This is usually caused by a state of great distress and can occasionally be an indicator of abuse. Staff will need to observe closely and to work hard to build up a relationship with both child and parent. If further observation suggests that there is cause for serious concern, the group should already have in place procedures to be followed, which will include contact with the local social services department. The NSPCC Child Protection Hotline is included in the addresses at the back of this book.

Above all, the pre-school will offer to children experiencing speech and language difficulties the invaluable support it offers to all children: opportunities to talk and opportunities to listen.

The equipment provided for children with specific medical conditions enriches the environment for all children. Adrienne has no special needs, but enjoys using the support chair.

Children with ongoing medical conditions

Jon has haemophilia, which means that his blood does not clot in the ordinary way and quite minor cuts and bumps can be serious and even life-threatening for him. His parents have worked hard to keep him safe but Jon has now reached a stage where he needs the stimulus of other children and the health visitor has suggested that he should attend his local pre-school. His parents are torn. They want whatever is best for Jon but they are fearful about the risks and reluctant to entrust their son to other people. Jon's mother arranges to bring him to the pre-school for a visit. It is immediately clear that Jon, although rather shy with the other children, is absolutely delighted by the pre-school activities. He is soon busy with paint and glue, though he keeps one eye on his mother. The pre-school leader is quick to assure Jon's mother that she and/or Jon's father will always be welcome in the pre-school and that their presence will help him to settle into the group and feel comfortable there. Their presence will be especially valuable, the pre-school leader goes on to say, because the group will need the help and advice of his parents in creating a safe and suitable environment for Jon. She outlines the adjustments they have already planned to make if Jon joins them, such as padding around the corners of tables, and asks what else they ought to do. The fact that the group has already given thought to Jon's special needs begins to reassure his mother. She agrees to stay till the end of the session, when she can go round the premises and equipment with the pre-school leader and chair and conduct a risk assessment with Jon's needs in mind.

Children's learning and development can be affected by a range of medical conditions. Some of these will mean that some children have additional or special needs. However, the needs which all children have in common are crucially important, and the ways in which they are met will determine the children's happiness, self-esteem and success. All children need access to rich and satisfying play experiences and to a graduated series of challenges which help them explore their full potential in all areas of their development. The pre-school may be involved, with advice from the child's doctor and parent, in helping to avoid or alleviate physical problems arising from the child's medical condition but will also be actively engaged in ensuring that the child experiences the full range of learning opportunities available in the pre-school.

Some parents feel so protective of their child that they find it hard to hand over the responsibility for the child's care and education, even for a short time. They need time to become familiar with the quality of the experiences and support which the pre-school can offer their child. During this acclimatisation period, which takes some parents longer than others, the parent's presence in the group can provide a useful additional resource.

In ensuring that the experiences offered in pre-school are suitable for the child, the community paediatric nurse or health visitor will be a valuable source of advice. S/he can be contacted via the local health centre or through the child's parents.

Some children may need to receive medication in pre-school. Groups must ensure that:

- They have the parent's written permission
- They seek professional medical advice where necessary
- Their insurance covers the administration of medication
- They have appropriate training – usually from the child's parents, from a health visitor or from the local community paediatric nurse
- More than one member of staff is involved – this ensures that one adult can monitor the work of another and that they can stand in for one another where necessary.

Children with severe allergy

A severe allergic reaction is one in which the whole body is affected by a very small amount of the trigger substance. These may occur in food – especially peanuts – but can also be present in some drugs or in the stings of some insects.

A child having an allergic reaction may experience changes in heartbeat, swelling, cramps, sudden lassitude and difficulties in breathing and swallowing/speaking. If a child has been diagnosed as suffering from severe allergic reaction, staff will know what symptoms to look for and may have been provided with medication – usually adrenalin in the form of an epi-pen which is very easy to use. It is possible however for the condition not to be diagnosed until the child encounters the allergen for the first time. The symptoms should be known to the adults, who should watch out for them in all children.

For children who have been diagnosed, the environment must be adjusted as necessary and with great care. Inclusion means making the activities suitable for each child, not merely excluding some children from some activities. It is not only resources provided in the group which can pose a risk to children with allergies, but snacks brought from home, or traces of food in packaging materials used for collage or in the house play area.

Children with severe asthma

During asthma attacks, reduced lung capacity gives rise to breathlessness and fatigue. These can be so severe that they in turn give rise to panic, which can worsen the initial symptoms and make the situation worse.

Many children with asthma, even very young children, carry their own medication with them to use at need. In some cases pre-school staff, in co-operation with parents, may be involved in helping them. Staff will also need to know what to do in the case of a major attack, and at what point to seek medical assistance.

Asthma can be triggered by allergic reactions, and parents will be able to give advice on the situations/substances which can bring on an attack in their child. An inclusive approach means that the child must be offered the full range of play and learning experiences in the pre-school, while avoiding the triggers. This may mean adapting the materials on offer to ensure that if, for example, the child is allergic to egg, cookery activities either exclude egg or offer alternatives.

Children who have been treated for cancer

Children who have undergone chemotherapy or radiotherapy may have damaged immune systems and will therefore be very vulnerable to infection. They will catch childhood illnesses more readily and be much more at risk from them than other children. The implications for practice within the group are two-fold:

- When a virus such as chicken-pox is present among the children in the group, all parents should be informed immediately
- A child who has frequent absences may miss some of the learning opportunities enjoyed by the other children. Staff will have to be alert to this so as to ensure that the child has extra chances to catch up on the days when s/he is present.

Children who have received extensive hospital treatment of any kind may want to talk about their experiences. Doctor and nurse outfits in the role play area, together with books about "people who help us" in hospital, can provide useful opportunities.

Staff will need to be more than usually attentive to these children's energy levels in order to protect them if necessary from becoming over-tired.

Children with cystic fibrosis

Thick mucus in the lungs gives rise to chest infections and breathing problems. Regular physiotherapy is necessary to keep the lungs functioning and to help the child to cough up secretions. Parents and/or physiotherapist will give any necessary instruction about this. Meanwhile, the pre-school will need to:

- Protect the child from sources of infection and from becoming cold or wet
- Check with the child's parents about any physical limitations on the child's activities
- Make sure that the full range of activities is available to the child, making adjustments as necessary. It may be useful to offer the child with cystic fibrosis the opportunity to do in a sitting-down position some activities which are normally conducted standing up. A shortened easel, for example, or paints on a low table, will enable the child to paint sitting down. Other children also may welcome this extension to the range of options available.

Children with diabetes

In this condition the child's body lacks insulin and is therefore unable to regulate blood sugar levels. The condition is controlled on an ongoing basis by medication and diet. Staff will need to maintain close links with home so that they can:

- Be aware of the child's dietary needs, exercising particular caution at snack time, during cookery activities and at parties (The "diabetic" label on some sweet products does not necessarily mean that the product is suitable for a particular person with diabetes.)
- Ensure that if the children are having food "treats", not all of them are sweet ones
- Be trained if appropriate to give regular medication
- While ensuring in the spirit of inclusion that the child has access to the full range of activities, be extra careful to avoid bumps and bruises which can give rise to infection.

In addition, if the blood sugar level goes out of control staff will need to recognise a diabetic crisis and to know what to do if it occurs. Here again close links with home will be necessary and clear medical advice.

Children with severe eczema

Eczema is severe dryness of the skin which leads to itchiness, cracking, weeping and scaling. The condition itself and the medicines used to control it can make the skin very thin and liable to infection, but eczema is not in itself an infectious complaint and cannot be spread to other people. It is very important that other people in the group, including other children and their parents, are helped to understand this. Eczema can be a very isolating complaint simply because symptoms can be conspicuous and alarming to other people. The child with eczema, like all other children, needs the reassurance that he or she is a valued member of the group.

Eczema can be triggered by allergic reactions and parents will advise on the substances which can trigger an attack in their child. The child needs to receive the full range of stimulus and opportunities for learning and it may be necessary to adjust provision to ensure that these are available while avoiding trigger situations. If sand is an irritant, for example, the child may welcome opportunities to play with substitutes. The salt in playdough also may be an irritant and it may be necessary to make available more kinds of playdough, including some without salt. Cotton gloves beside the dough and/or sand can make these activities accessible to some children with eczema and also to other children.

Children with epilepsy

This condition causes seizures or spasms, which can range from momentary blankness to spasmodic jerky movements which can lead to unconsciousness. The condition can be controlled by medication, though it can take time to achieve the correct balance of medication and this may need to be adjusted as the child develops. The nature and frequency of the seizures will determine the amount of special help the child needs in pre-school, but staff will need to discuss with parents what to do:

- Before a seizure, the time during which warning symptoms may be apparent
- During a seizure, when the child may need to be protected from bumping into things and adults will need to check whether the duration of the symptoms is normal for that child
- After a seizure, when the child may need opportunities to be quiet, comforted or sleepy.

Between seizures, the child needs access to all the activities in the pre-school. Close links with home will ensure that messages about the child's physical safety needs are passed on. Parents will provide information about medication. If the child needs to take regular medication, or if there are steps to be taken at the onset of a seizure, this information needs to be shared with more than one member of staff. If only the keyworker, for example, is aware of it, there is always a danger that he or she might not be present at the time when medication needs to be given.

In a few cases, there is a known trigger which can give rise to a seizure. This information also needs to be widely shared so that the child is not accidentally put at risk.

Children with haemophilia

In this condition the blood lacks the ingredient which makes it clot. This makes the healing of what would otherwise be minor damage very difficult, not just on the skin but also internally.

Discussion and close co-operation with parents is necessary to create an inclusive environment in which all learning activities are genuinely accessible to the child with the minimum of risk. This might involve padding corners and sharp edges on the furniture and devising energetic play activities which offer maximum physical exercise and challenge with minimum risk of accident.

In addition to creating an extra safe physical environment staff will also need to be alert for the symptoms of dangerous internal bleeding. Pallor, lassitude and dizziness might indicate a small internal injury which is putting the child at risk and medical advice must be sought straight away.

Inclusion
in pre-school settings

Children with hepatitis

Children with HIV

All forms of hepatitis are dangerous and the disease is communicable. It affects the functioning of the blood and liver. Hepatitis A gives rise to a fever, which continues for a long time. Hepatitis B causes liver damage and hinders the body's immune response. Hepatitis C can lead to a carrier state in which the person with the disease is without symptoms but can transmit it to other people.

Because the presence of a carrier may not be known, the only safe way to behave is to assume that a carrier is present:

- All spillages of blood and bodily fluids must be cleared immediately using a chlorine or iodine bleach diluted according to manufacturer's instructions.
- People dealing with blood or bodily fluids should wear disposable rubber gloves, which must be available at all times in the group.
- Items which have saliva on them – which can often happen where very young children are present – should be washed in very hot water.
- Open cuts and sores should be covered.

These safeguards will protect all members of the group from any possibility of infection and make it unnecessary for anybody other than the keyworker and/or pre-school leader to know that a particular child is infected.

Immunisation is possible if a known carrier or infected person is present.

This disease is less easily communicated than hepatitis. It is similar however in that people may be infected and in a position to pass on the disease without anybody – including themselves – being necessarily aware of the fact. The only way to proceed in a group situation therefore is to behave as though an infected person were present:

- All open wounds and sores to be covered
- All spillages of blood and bodily fluids to be cleaned immediately, using bleach diluted according to manufacturer's instructions and wearing disposable gloves for the purpose
- Articles with saliva on them washed in hot water.

If a child in the group is known to be infected with HIV, staff will need to work hard to ensure that:

- Any other children and adults in the group who know of the situation understand that the hygiene precautions described above ensure that nobody else will catch it. This is very important because one of the unnecessary results of HIV infection is social isolation which can be additionally damaging to a child
- Because the child is very vulnerable to infection, her/his parents are alerted immediately if childhood illnesses such as chicken-pox are present in the group
- The child receives necessary support in catching up on play and learning experiences he or she misses during what may be frequent absences due to illness
- In discussion with parents, confidentiality is maintained, information being passed only to those who need to know.

Children with hydrocephalus

Children who have received organ transplants

This condition sometimes occurs at the same time as spina bifida. It happens when the fluid around the brain does not drain properly and the build-up of fluid causes pressure and damage to the brain. Usually, a "shunt" is inserted to provide drainage and this works effectively so long as it does not become blocked or the site infected. However, the initial build-up of pressure may have caused some damage to the brain before the shunt is inserted. This can give rise to problems with attention span and will make it doubly important that the pre-school activities are geared to the child's stage rather than chronological age.

Close links with parents to establish the child's specific needs and abilities will ensure that:

- Appropriate head protection is worn if necessary
- All staff in the group know what to look for so that any blockage in the shunt is recognised rapidly. In particular, staff will be alert for raised temperature and sudden lassitude.

If the transplant has been effective, these children can be very exciting to work with, as they are feeling healthier, perhaps, than they have in their lives before and are eager for all the learning opportunities pre-school has to offer.

Staff will need to work closely with parents to ensure that the children's specific needs are met and that any risk of infection is avoided. Parents will be a source of advice on keeping the child safe and comfortable. It may be necessary, for example, to offer drinks more frequently than usual.

If the child needs to use a naso-gastric tube, the group, in addition to working closely with parents and medical advisers, must check the position with insurers and with the registering authority.

Children with the after-effects of poliomyelitis

Children with sickle cell disease/thalassaemia

Polio is a viral infection which affects the intestinal lining, blood stream and central nervous system. The illness in itself is dangerous but it can also give rise to long-term paralysis/muscle weakness. Children who have survived polio therefore may need help in coping with these after-effects. Polio is less common than it used to be because of the widespread and highly successful immunisation programme.

The child who has recovered from polio is no longer ill and needs access to the full range of learning activities offered by the pre-school. Some of these may need to be adapted to ensure inclusion if the child wears leg braces or has pronounced muscular weakness. Such a child may need a different route around obstacle courses and the opportunity to sit down if necessary for activities, such as painting and water play, which are often done in a standing position. Opportunities must be created for the child to exercise the upper body without needing agility in the lower limbs if these have been weakened.

In this chronic blood disorder, the blood does not flow or carry oxygen efficiently. People with these disorders suffer aches and pains – not necessarily minor ones – and great fatigue. They are also prone to infection, which may result in frequent absence from pre-school.

In a sickle cell crisis, the child slows down very considerably and experiences great pain and high temperature leading to collapse.

Staff will need to work closely with parents to ensure that any ongoing medication is taken and also to ensure that crisis medication is available if necessary. The child needs encouragement to take plenty of fluid. Drinks should be available – and offered – when necessary, not just at general meal or snack times.

The child also needs access to the full range of pre-school experiences and an inclusive approach means that the group may have to adjust its provision in order to make this possible. The fatigue and discomfort suffered by children with sickle cell disease mean that physical activities in particular may have to be adapted in order to allow them to take part. An obstacle course, for example, may need to be shortened. In addition, the child's frequent absences may mean that he or she needs opportunities to catch up on learning experiences which the other children have already had.

Children with spina bifida

In this condition a break in the spinal column before birth exposes the central nervous column and may limit the function of limbs and parts of the body below the break. The pre-school will need to make practical adjustments, working in co-operation with the child's family, to ensure that:

- If the child's bladder or bowel function is affected, the pre-school can cope with whatever systems the child needs to use, whether this involves nappies, potties, bags to be emptied, or a combination of these
- If there are some children who operate most comfortably at floor level or who pull themselves along the floor, the floor surfaces are smooth and safe
- The environment is adapted as necessary to ensure that these children have full access to all learning opportunities; this might involve making some activities available at ground level
- If the child is mobile by means of a wheelchair, the chair is used for mobility purposes and the child does not remain in it at other times, which can be unnecessarily limiting
- The child has plenty of opportunities to exercise the parts of the body which are not affected by the condition
- Links are made and maintained where appropriate with the physiotherapist and/or occupational therapist, who will be able to advise on keeping the child safe and comfortable by means of correct positioning and possibly special seating.

Children with chronic medical conditions, like all other children, need a pre-school environment within which they can enjoy the fun and satisfaction of exploring and developing their full potential in company with their peers and with friendly, supportive adults. In a setting with an inclusive approach, the environment will be adjusted as necessary to ensure that all children have the opportunity to be included in all activities.

Holly likes the challenge of getting to the top.

Other conditions which may give rise to learning difficulties

Lesley goes nowhere without a particular red plastic mug, which she clutches throughout the pre-school session. Occasionally she talks to it. She will not relinquish it to take up any other activity. It is clear to the staff that the learning opportunities they want to offer Lesley are going to have to reach her by means of the plastic mug. Lesley is good at counting, so they begin by counting a series of coloured beads into the mug as she holds it. Later she is encouraged to use the mug to scoop up dry sand to pour through the sand wheel. In the sound corner, a range of materials such as milk-bottle tops and acorns are placed in the mug so that she can discover the sounds they make when she shakes it. Once she feels confident about using her mug in this way, she becomes willing to let go of it for long enough for it to be weighed on the balance with and without dry sand inside it.

Many different conditions and situations can give rise to learning difficulties, and these can affect children in a variety of ways. For children with learning difficulties therefore, as for any other group of children, there is no single approach which will work for all of them. The good practice which informs the work of the pre-school as a whole is doubly important for children who have special educational needs:

- Observe the child, in order to establish accurately what has already been achieved and what the child could go on to next.

- On the basis of observation, decide what additional support may be necessary. Some children benefit from one-to-one adult attention. Others may not need the same level of individual attention, but may require the presence of an extra adult in the group to ensure that the rich and stimulating environment needed by some children does not threaten the safety of others. (For example, if some children are sufficiently skilful and experienced to need small and detailed constructional equipment such as Meccano or technical Lego, and others are at the stage of putting all small objects in their mouths, extra adult time will be needed to satisfy the needs of both groups.)

- Give parents the kind and level of support they want. Some parents, if their children have learning difficulties, need the company and advice of groups of other parents; others prefer a more private approach. In either case, the group can help.

There are many conditions which can give rise to learning difficulties and not all of them will be formally diagnosed. Some parents may be told that their child has "developmental delay" without knowing what to expect or how to help the child. Pre-schools which aim for an inclusive approach will be observing each child on an individual basis. This will enable staff to understand the child's current level of achievement in all areas of development and to go on from there to plan fresh targets and new challenges.

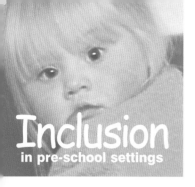

Children with autistic spectrum disorder

Children who have one of the range of autistic spectrum disorders will have difficulty in communicating with and relating to other people. They may be very slow to speak, or speak in a very expressionless way, without smiles, eye contact or any sign of interest in or affection for other people.

When looking at people or objects, these children tend to concentrate on isolated features rather than the whole thing: they will focus on an item of clothing rather than the person wearing it, or one button on the doll's dress rather than the whole doll. This limits their opportunity to use objects symbolically in play, and they often show very limited signs of imagination.

Children on the autistic spectrum have difficulty in recognising appropriateness in all sorts of social situations, including gesture, tone of voice and even selection of food materials. Adults can help by accompanying speech and language by appropriate gestures in order to help the children to understand gesture and use it appropriately.

Children with autistic spectrum disorders seek pattern in their lives and in the events around them. They often impose patterns themselves in the form of repetitive behaviours such as rocking, walking on their toes or touching particular objects repeatedly. The pre-school can help by providing a predictable routine and giving them plenty of time to learn to recognise the features of the pre-school session.

The children may need help in handling strange food fads as well as an unusual degree of thirstiness.

Because autistic spectrum disorders make it very hard for children to recognise what is appropriate in social situations, the children may very well need one-to-one adult support during structured sessions such as circle time or snack time in groups. Some children respond more readily to music than to spoken words. They may take great pleasure in singing time, perhaps responding especially well to particular songs, and may also find it easier to respond to sung instructions than to spoken ones.

Like all children, children with autistic spectrum disorders will benefit from standard good practice:

- Celebrating with the child any achievement
- Breaking down long-term goals into small, attainable steps
- Close observation. In the case of autistic spectrum disorder, this will enable the adults to recognise patterns in the child's behaviour and come to understand what experiences build pleasure and confidence and which ones may make the child afraid or distressed.

Children with autistic spectrum disorder can be a source of great anxiety to their parents and some parents will have established a particular set of techniques for handling the child. These may not always coincide with the approaches used in the group, and a shared approach must be discussed with parents before the child is admitted.

Children with Down's syndrome

Because these children are so easy to recognise, it is very easy to make wholly inappropriate assumptions about them. Children with Down's syndrome have widely varying abilities and personalities, just like any other group of children, and must be observed to ensure that their individual needs are met.

Children with Down's syndrome often have poor muscle tone. This can be improved by exercise, and a physiotherapist will advise on activities which will develop the children's gross motor development as well as fine motor control. Some children with Down's syndrome may suffer heart and chest conditions which need particular handling. The child's parents will be the best source of advice on any specific steps that need to be taken to keep the child safe and comfortable.

Down's syndrome will result in developmental milestones being delayed, but by varying degrees. Only close observation will identify the current achievements of any particular child and appropriate targets for that child to move on to.

Children with Down's syndrome have large tongues which can make speech production hard for them. Speech therapy and singing can make an enormous difference. The exercises which assist the development of clear speech will also help them overcome problems in eating and drinking. Makaton signing is very helpful for children with Down's syndrome and usually gets an enthusiastic response from all the children in the group. It needs to be used by all staff and taught to all children so that the children can communicate with one another.

Children with Down's syndrome want and need to join in with the group, to be challenged by new activities and helped to take a responsible part in the life of the group. In order to achieve inclusion, the support of a one-to-one adult helper may be useful for some children, but not all children with Down's syndrome need this.

For these children, as for all children, it is important for the group to work closely with the parents to share and record the child's achievements.

Children with rare chromosome disorders

Children can be affected by a range of uncommon chromosome disorders. These all have different effects upon the children and the only way to help is to promote good practice:

- Work closely with the parents and where appropriate with medical and advisory services
- Observe the child closely
- Break down the long-term curriculum into short, attainable steps
- Celebrate all achievements, however small
- Make sure that parents as well as the group are able to plug in to all available statutory and voluntary support services.

Families whose child has a very unusual condition can sometimes feel extremely isolated. Often the most valuable source of help is another family dealing with the same issues and concerns. Contact with other families can be made by means of organisations such as UNIQUE, In Touch and Contact a Family. The addresses of these organisations are at the end of the book.

Everybody needs the opportunity to tackle difficult jobs -
including getting socks back on after a session in the ball pool.

The exceptionally able child

Ramon has been making an elaborate construction with the technical Lego. He is upset when the activity comes to an end before he has finished it to his satisfaction and he is required to join the other children for story time. The story fails to hold his attention and he begins to seek other occupation – firstly by drumming with his feet on the legs of his chair and then by attempting to attract the attention of the child sitting next to him, who is engrossed in the story. Eventually, Ramon's keyworker suggests that as Ramon already knows this story, he should sit beside the adult who is reading to the children and help her by selecting the appropriate felt shapes and mounting them on the felt board, to illustrate the story for the other children as the tale progresses. This works as a short-term measure, but it is clear to the staff that if Ramon, as well as the other children, is to be helped to see books as a source of delight, they are going to have to provide him with more appropriate texts and to re-think the way they organise story time.

Children who are unusually able do not fall within the category of "special educational needs" as defined by the Code of Practice and indeed most parents are pleased when their children show particular abilities and want to encourage them. However, children who are exceptionally able can be as challenging to work with as children who have difficulties in learning. A child who seems already to have progressed beyond the pre-school curriculum, or who asks very difficult questions, can be threatening or daunting to some adults. In addition, a child whose learning needs are not being met may have become restless and dissatisfied even before he or she enters pre-school and may therefore appear to present behavioural difficulties as well as intellectual challenges.

Children with exceptional ability need the same things as other children:

- A broad and balanced curriculum
- New challenges, in all areas of their development
- Respect and attention because they are what they are, not just for what they can do.

The first rule, as with all children, is to observe. Some exceptionally able children seem to develop rapidly in all areas, but many others have exceptional talents in one or two areas and have no exceptional skills, or even perhaps difficulties, in other areas. The child's needs cannot be met until close observation has indicated clearly what they are. If the child has exceptional ability in one particular area, such as mathematics, it may be necessary to provide additional equipment which will offer more sophisticated challenges. When such equipment is provided in a pre-school, it almost always serves to enrich the curriculum, not just for that one child, but for many other children in the group.

A child whose development is very uneven needs additional support and opportunities to develop in areas he or she finds less easy. Children who are already competent at reading or writing may be in great need of opportunities to develop gross motor skills on wheeled vehicles or climbing and scrambling equipment. Children who show advanced mathematical ability may need more opportunities to develop their imaginative and responsive play, in the home play area and also with paints and other mark-making equipment. For all children it is essential that they be given practice and support in developing social skills and in learning to respect and value one another.

Contacts
The addresses of support groups, including the National Association for Gifted Children and the National Association for Able Children in Education, are included at the end of this book.

The sand at floor level is accessible to children who cannot stand at a sand tray, but it also provides fun for Joseph and his mother.

Links with other bodies

Neither children nor pre-schools operate in a vacuum. The group will need to work with other organisations in order to achieve the best possible quality of support for the child. In addition, groups can perform a valuable service by creating links between families and a range of other organisations which can support them.

For parents whose child has a special educational need, there are now systems of "parent partnerships" in which people are trained to provide independent support through the statementing process. If this resource is available locally, knowledge of it can be very valuable to some parents. The Government is supporting this initiative and hopes eventually to make it available more widely and at an earlier stage. The National Network of Parent Partnership Schemes publishes regular newsletters and can provide contact numbers for local schemes. Their address is at the end of the book.

Links with statutory bodies

Voluntary bodies

In order to meet the needs of a particular child and family, the group will frequently need to work in close partnership with staff from the local education, social services or health departments. It is very useful if groups can be sure that they know in advance who the key professionals are in each department, who can be contacted and how. It is useful to keep a record of the names and addresses of local contacts (dated, ideally, so it is easy to check if they go out of date).

Linked with lists of personnel are indications of resources available locally. Sometimes particular staff are able to tap particular funding sources. In other areas, there may be access to a specialist toy library or to the services of educational psychologists, speech therapists and paediatric specialists.

The Early Years Development & Childcare Partnerships (EYDCPs) can be very useful in this respect. All EYDCP plans contain information on how children with special educational needs are to be supported within the partnership. Pre-School Learning Alliance representatives on these bodies can make themselves responsible for asking exactly what is available, to whom and how.

Once a group is approached by a family whose child has a special need, it is very much easier for both group and family if the contact names and indications of support are all ready to hand.

Everybody knows that there are numbers of voluntary organisations supporting children and families experiencing specific difficulties or disabilities. However, it is not always easy to find out exactly which bodies are active in any particular locality. It is very useful for parents if the group can keep track of what is available. The local library is a good starting point. There are usually telephone numbers there of some local organisations and very frequently it is possible to find out about more organisations by ringing one of them. If the group displays leaflets from local support organisations of all kinds, this provides an invaluable resource for parents. It can be particularly helpful for parents who have just been told, or who are just beginning themselves to suspect, that their child has a special need. They can then "plug in" quickly to a source of practical and specific expertise, support and understanding.

Insurance

Support organisations

All pre-schools need insurance and the insurance, like the group's other areas of activity, should be inclusive. Look for an insurance policy which covers children with and without special educational needs. There are policies which provide less cover for some children by excluding those with a "pre-disposing condition". The policy negotiated between the Pre-school Learning Alliance and the Royal & SunAlliance has no such exclusion clause and all children in the group are included in the cover without the need for any special notification, on condition that medical advice and the insurer's guidelines are followed as appropriate.

The list which begins on page 52 is not, and could never be, fully comprehensive. However, it does aim to give a national contact address and telephone number for support organisations covering most kinds of disability and learning difficulty. Parents – or groups – in need of support and advice can contact the national body and will then be told if there is a local branch available – or, in some cases, given advice on how to start one.

Every effort has been made to ensure that this list is accurate. If any reader has news of changes, or suggestions for any further edition, please contact the Alliance at the number on the back cover and ask to speak to the Editor. We will be most grateful for your help.

Parents are an invaluable resource. Joseph's mother helps Grace work with the computer.

Further reading

Advisory Centre for Education (1996)
**Special Education Handbook:
the law on children with special needs**
ACE Publications, London
Encourages parents to become informed about and involved
in decisions about their children's education by describing
in non-technical language the way the law requires relevant
agencies to help and support children and young people
with special educational needs.

Allez A, Arnott J, Henderson A and Toff M (1996)
Equal Chances
Pre-school Learning Alliance
Eliminating discrimination and ensuring equality
in pre-schools

Bender M and Henderson A (1997)
**Children with Special Needs in Pre-schools:
having regard to the DfEE Code of Practice**
Pre-school Learning Alliance
The practical implications of the Code for people working
in pre-school settings

Dickins & Denziloe (1998)
**How to Create Inclusive Services for Disabled
Children and their Families**
National Early Years Network
Useful and practical guidance for groups wanting to move
towards inclusive policies.

Gascoigne, E. (1995)
**Working with Parents as Partners in Special
Educational Needs**
Fulton, London
The role of parents in helping a child with special
educational needs to achieve her or his
fullest potential

Hobart & Frankel
Practical Guide to Child Observation
Stanley Thorne
The principles and practice of child observation, useful for
staff in all pre-schools and for students on childcare courses

Henderson A et al (1994)
**Observation and Record-keeping:
a curriculum for each child**
Pre-school Learning Alliance
Techniques for observing children, plus photocopiable
records to share with parents

Lear, R (1977)
Play Helps and **More Play Helps**
Heinemann Medical
A very practical and accessible approach to toys and play
activities which many parents have found useful

McDowell, D (Ed)
**HIV and Children Under Five:
a guide for workers and carers**
George House Trust
A practical guide to help staff and carers ensure good
practice when working with children with HIV

Robson, B (1989)
**Pre-school Provision for Children with
Special Needs**
Cassell, London
Describes in plain language how to provide for children
with special needs in pre-school so as to ensure that the
children enjoy and learn from their experiences there

Spencer, C & Schnelling, K (1998)
**Handbook for Pre-school Special Educational Needs
Provision: The Code of Practice in relation to the
early years**
Fulton, London
Provides a guide through the statutory assessment process
for adults working with children in a range of settings.
Photocopiable materials for use in the assessment process
are valuable also for collaborative use by parents and
group workers.

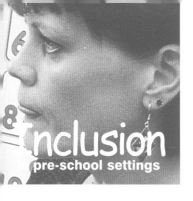

Organisations which support families with special needs

Action for Sick Children
300 Kingston Road
Wimbledon
London SW20 8LX
Tel: 0171 833 2041

Attention Deficit [Hyperactive] Disorder (ADD/ADHD) Support Group
44 Drynham Road
Trowbridge
Wilts BA14 0PE

Advisory Centre for Education (ACE)
Unit 1B, Aberdeen Studios
22 Highbury Grove
London N5 2DQ
Tel: 0171 354 8321

Arthritis Care
18 Stephenson Way
London NW1 2HD
Tel: 0171 916 1500

AFASIC (Association For All Speech Impaired Children)
69-85 Old Street
London EC1V 9HX
Tel: 0171 841 8900

Anaphylaxis Campaign
PO Box 149
Fleet
Hampshire GU13 9XU
01252 542 029

Association for Brain Damaged Children
Clifton House
3 St. Paul's Road, Foleshill
Coventry CV6 5DE
Tel: 01203 665 450

Association for Spina Bifida and Hydrocephalus
ASBAH House, 42 Park Road
Peterborough PE1 2UQ
Tel: 01733 555 988

British Diabetic Association
10 Queen Anne Street
London W1M 0BD
Tel: 0171 323 1531

British Dyslexia Association
98 London Road
Reading RG1 5AU
Tel: 0118 966 8271

British Epilepsy Association
Anstey House
40 Hanover Square
Leeds LS3 1BE
Tel: 0113 243 9393

British Institute for Learning Disability
Wolverhampton Road
Kidderminster DY10 3PP
Tel: 01562 850 251

British Stammerers' Association
15 Old Ford Road
London
E2 9PJ
Tel: 0181 983 1003

Brittle Bone Society
30 Guthrie Street
Dundee DD1 5BS
Tel: 01382 204 446

Centre for Studies on Inclusive Education
1 Redland Close
Elm Lane, Redland
Bristol BS6 6UE
Tel: 0117 923 8450

Child Psychotherapy Trust (CPT)
Star House
104-108 Grafton Road
London NW5 4BD
Tel: 0171 284 1355

Clear Vision
Lindon Lodge School
61 Princes Way
London SW19 6JB

Contact a Family
170 Tottenham Court Road
London W1P 0HA
Tel: 0171 383 3555

Council for Disabled Children
8 Wakley Street
London EC1V 7QE
Tel: 0171 843 6000

Cystic Fibrosis Research Trust
11 London Road
Bromley
Kent BR1 1BY
Tel: 0181 464 7211

Deaf Education through Listening and Talking (DELTA)
PO Box 20, Haverhill
Suffolk CB9 7BD
Tel: 01440 783 689

Defeating Deafness
330-332 Gray's Inn Road
London
WC1X 8EE
Tel: 0171 833 1733

Developmental Dyspraxia Foundation
8 West Alley
Hitchin S65 1EG
Tel: 01462 454 986

Dial UK – The Disability Helpline
(Nationwide telephone information and advice services)
Park Lodge,
St Catherine's Hospital
Tickhill Road, Doncaster DN4 8QN
Tel: 01302 310 123.

Disability Alliance, ERC
(Publish Disability Rights Handbook)
Universal House
88-94 Wentworth Street
London E1 7SA
Tel: 0171 247 8776

Disabled Living Foundation
380-384 Harrow Road
London W9 2HU
Tel: 0171 289 6111

Down's Syndrome Association
155 Mitcham Road
London SW17 9PG
Tel: 0181 682 4001

Dyslexia Institute
133 Gresham Road
Staines
Middlesex TW18 2AJ
Tel: 01784 463 851

European Council for High Ability
C/o Professor Joan Freeman
21 Montagu Square
London W1H 1RE
0171 486 2604

Family Fund Trust
PO Box 50
York YO1 9ZX.
Tel: 01904 621 115

Foundation for the Study of Infant Deaths
14 Halkin Street,
London SW1X 7DP
Tel: 0171 235 1721

Friedreich's Ataxia Group
The Stable, Wiggins Yard
Bridge Street, Godalming
Surrey GU7 1HW
Tel: 01483 417 111

Greater London Association for Disabled People (GLAD)
336 Brixton Road
London SW9 7AA
Tel: 0171 346 5800

Haemophilia Society
3rd Floor, Chesterfield House
385 Euston Road
London NW1 3AU
Tel: 0171 380 0600

HAPA (formerly Handicapped Adventure Playgroup Assoc.)
Pryor's Bank, Bishops Park
London SW6 3LA
Tel: 0171 736 4443

Home-Start UK
2 Salisbury Road
Leicester LE1 7QR
Tel: 0116 233 9955

Huntington's Disease Association
108 Battersea High Street
London SW11 3HP
Tel: 0171 223 7000

Hyperactive Children's Support Group
71 Whyke Lane, Chichester
Sussex PO19 2LD
Tel: 01903 725 182

In Touch
(For information and contacts on rare conditions)
10 Norman Road, Sale
Cheshire M33 3DF
Tel: 0161 905 2440

I CAN: Invalid Children's Aid Nationwide
4 Dyer's Buildings
Holborn
London EC1N 2QP
Tel: 0870 010 4066

Lady Hoare Trust for Physically Disabled Children
87 Worship Street
London EC2A 2BE
Tel: 0171 377 7567

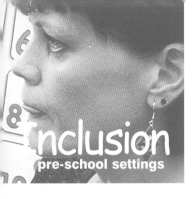

Leukaemia Care Society
14 Kingfisher Court
Venny Bridge
Pinhoe, Exeter
Devon EX4 8JN
Tel: 01392 464 848

Letterbox Library
Unit 2d
Leroy House
436 Essex road
London N1 3QP

**Makaton Vocabulary
Development Project**
31 Firwood Drive
Camberley
Surrey GU15 3QD
Tel: 01276 61390

MENCAP
(Royal Society for Mentally
Handicapped Children and Adults)
117-123 Golden Lane
London EC1Y 0RF
Tel: 0171 454 0454

MIND
(National Association for Mental Health)
15-19 Broadway
London E15 4BQ
Tel: 0181 519 2122

Motability
Goodman House
Station Approach, Harlow
Essex CM20 2ET
Tel: 01279 635 999

**Muscular Dystrophy Group of
Great Britain**
7-11 Prescott Place
London SW4 6BS
Tel: 0171 720 8055

National Autistic Society
393 City Road
London EC1V 1NG
Tel: 0171 833 2299

**National Association for Able
Children in Education**
Westminster College
Oxford
OX2 AT
01865 245657

**National Association for
Gifted Children**
Elder House
Milton Keynes
MK9 1LR
01908 673667

**National Association of
Hospital Play Staff**
Fladgate
Forty Green
Beaconsfield HP9 1XS

**National Association of Toy and
Leisure Libraries** (Play Matters)
68 Churchway
London NW1 1LT
Tel: 0171 387 9592

National Deaf Children's Society
15 Dufferin Street
London EC1Y 8PD
Tel: 0171 490 8656

National Eczema Society
163 Eversholt Street
London NW1 1BU
Tel: 0171 388 4097

**National Network of Parent
Partnership Schemes**
Council for Disabled Children
National Children's Bureau
8 Wakely Street
London EC1V 7QE
Tel: 0171 278 9512

National Portage Association
127 Monks Dale, Yeovil
Somerset BA21 3JE
Tel: 01935 471 641

Network 81
1-7 Woodfield Terrace
Stansted
Essex CM24 8AJ
Tel: 01279 647 415

**NSPCC Child
Protection Hotline**
0800 800500

Parents for Inclusion
Unit 2, 70 South Lambeth Road
London SW8 1RL
Tel: 0171 735 7735

PHAB England
(Physically Disabled and Able Bodied)
Summit House
Wandle Road
Croydon, Surrey CR0 1DF
Tel: 0181 667 9443

PLANET
(Play Leisure Advice Network)
Save the Children
Cambridge House
Cambridge Grove
London W6 0LE
Tel: 0181 741 4119

REACH
(National Resource Centre for Children
with Reading Difficulties)
Wellington House
Wellington Street
Wokingham RG11 2AG
Tel: 01734 891 101

**Royal Association for Disability &
Rehabilitation (RADAR)**
12 City Forum
250 City Road
London EC1V 8AF
Tel: 0171 250 3222

**Royal College of Speech &
Language Therapists**
(Send SAE for information)
7 Bath Place
London EC2A 3SU

**Royal National Institute for
Deaf People**
19-23 Featherstone Street
London EC1Y 8SL
Tel: 0171 296 8000

SCOPE
(formerly Spastics Society)
6 Market Road
London N7 9PW
Tel: 0171 619 7100

SENSE
The National Deafblind & Rubella
Association
11-13 Clifton Terrace
Finsbury Park
London N4 3SR
Tel: 0171 272 7774

Sickle Cell Society
54 Station Road
London NW10 4UA
Tel: 0181 961 7795

Spinal Injuries Association
76 St James Lane
London N10 3DF
Tel: 0181 444 2121

Terrence Higgins Trust
52-54 Gray's Inn Road
London WC1X 8JU
Tel: 0171 831 0330

Tuberous Sclerosis Association
Little Barnsley Farm
Catshil, Bromsgrove
Worcs B61 0NQ
Tel: 01527 871 898

UNIQUE
(for support and information on rare
chromosome abnormalities)
Edna Knight
160 Locket Road
Harrow Weald
Middlesex HA3 7MZ

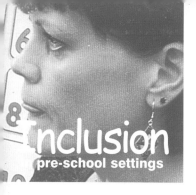

References

Bernthal, J E & Bankson, N W (1993)
Articulation and Phonological Disorder (3rd edition)
Englewood Cliffs, NJ: Prentice Hall

Beukelman, D R & Mirenda, P (1992)
Augmentative and Alternative Communication:
management of severe communication disorder
in children and adults
Baltimore, MD: Paul H Brookes

Centre for Studies on Inclusive Education (1997)
Inclusive Education:
the right to belong to the mainstream
CSIE, Bristol

Dare, A and OiDonovan, M (1997)
Good Practice in Caring for
Children with Special Needs
Stanley Thorne, London

Department of Education and Science (1989)
Discipline in Schools (The Elton Report)
HMSO, London

Department for Education (1994a)
Code of Practice on the Identification and Assessment
of Children with Special educational Needs
HMSO, London

Department for Education (1994b)
Pupil Behaviour and Discipline
(Circular 8/94)

Department for Education (1994c)
The Education of Children with Emotional and
Behavioural Difficulties
(Circular 9/94)

Fogell, J & Long, R (1997)
Emotional and Behavioural Difficulties
NASEN Publication, Stafford

Freeman, J (Ed) (1998)
Educating the Very Able:
current international research
The Stationery Office, London

Friedman, R J & Doyal, G T (1992)
Management of Children and Adolescents with
Attention Deficit Hyperactivity Disorder (3rd edition)
Pro-ed, Texas

Garner, P & Gains, C (1996)
Models of Intervention for Children with Emotional
and Behavioural Difficulties,
in Support for Learning, 11 (4), 141-145

Griffiths, A (Ed) (1999)
Dyspraxia,
in Special! Supporting and Developing Good Practice
Spring 1999, 16-19
Hobsons, Cambridge

SCOPE (1997)
When your child has cerebral palsy